SCOTLAND

Alice Harman

WAYLAND

FACT CAT

Get your paws on this fantastic new mega-series from Wayland!

Join our Fact Cat on a journey of fun learning about every subject under the sun!

First published in 2014 by Wayland
© Wayland 2014

Wayland
Hachette Children's Books
338 Euston Road
London NW1 3BH

Wayland Australia
Level 17/207 Kent Street
Sydney NSW 2000

Produced for Wayland by
White-Thomson Publishing Ltd
www.wtpub.co.uk
+44 (0) 843 208 7460

Editor: Alice Harman
Design: Rocket Design (East Anglia) Ltd
Fact Cat illustrations: Shutterstock/Julien Troneur
Other illustrations: Stefan Chabluk
Consultant: Kate Ruttle

A catalogue for this title is available from the British Library

ISBN: 978 0 7502 8439 4
ebook ISBN: 978 0 7502 8558 2

Dewey Number: 914.1'1-dc23

10 9 8 7 6 5 4 3 2 1

Wayland is a division of Hachette Children's Books,
an Hachette UK company.
www.hachette.co.uk

Printed and bound in China

The author, Alice Harman, is a writer and editor specialising in children's educational publishing.

The consultant, Kate Ruttle, is a literacy expert and SENCO, and teaches in Suffolk.

FACT CAT FACT

There is a question for you to answer on each spread in this book. You can check your answers on page 24.

CONTENTS

Welcome to Scotland...........4

Cities.....................6

The Highlands................8

Islands.....................10

Food.......................12

Wildlife....................14

Festivals...................16

Famous people...............18

Sport......................20

Quiz......................22

Glossary...................23

Index.....................24

Answers....................24

WELCOME TU SCOTLAND

Scotland is part of the United Kingdom, which is also called the UK. The other countries in the United Kingdom are England, Wales and Northern Ireland.

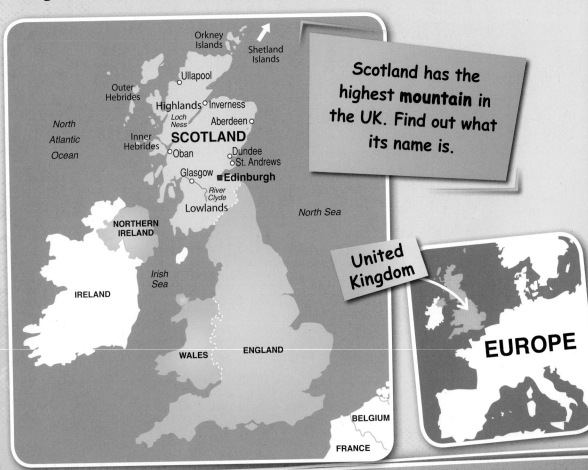

Orkney Islands

Shetland Islands

Ullapool

Outer Hebrides

Highlands Inverness

North Atlantic Ocean

Loch Ness

Aberdeen

Inner Hebrides

SCOTLAND

Oban

Dundee
St. Andrews

Glasgow ■Edinburgh

River Clyde

Lowlands

North Sea

NORTHERN IRELAND

Irish Sea

IRELAND

WALES

ENGLAND

BELGIUM

FRANCE

Scotland has the highest **mountain** in the UK. Find out what its name is.

United Kingdom

EUROPE

Edinburgh is the **capital** city of Scotland. It is a beautiful city, which is built on seven hills. It has many old buildings, including churches and **museums**.

Edinburgh Castle is built on part of a very old **volcano**, which has been **extinct** for a long time. Kings and queens used to live in the castle.

FACT CAT FACT

Every year, around 1.2 million people visit Edinburgh Castle. That's more than twice the number of people who actually live in Edinburgh!

CITIES

Although Edinburgh is the capital city of Scotland, Glasgow is the largest city in the country. The River Clyde runs through Glasgow.

People in Glasgow have another name for the Clyde Arc bridge. Can you find out what it is?

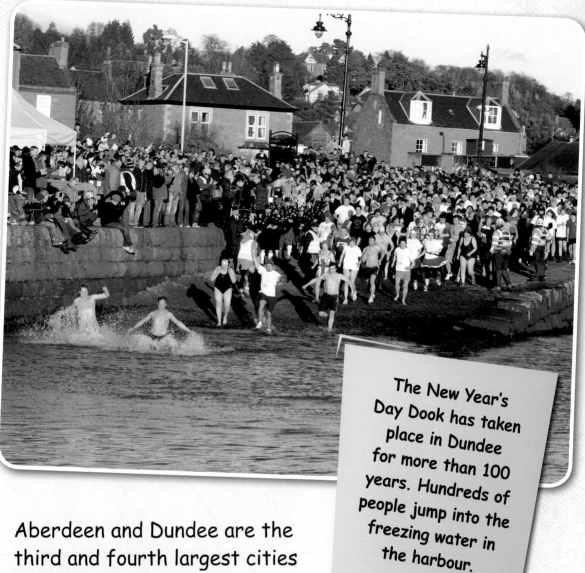

The New Year's Day Dook has taken place in Dundee for more than 100 years. Hundreds of people jump into the freezing water in the harbour.

Aberdeen and Dundee are the third and fourth largest cities in Scotland. They are both on the east coast. Aberdeen still has a very busy **harbour**, with 9000 boats each year travelling to 47 different countries.

THE HIGHLANDS

The Highlands is a large area of northern Scotland that has lots of mountains and hills. Not many people live in the Highlands, so **tourists** like to come and see the area's natural beauty.

Highland cattle are a **traditional** Scottish breed of cow. Find out which colours their **coats** can be.

Scotland has more than 31,000 lochs. A loch is a Scottish word for a lake. Most of Scotland's lochs are in the Highlands.

Loch Leven is a sea loch, which means it contains water from the sea.

FACT CAT FACT

Loch Ness is Scotland's biggest loch, and some people think a monster lives in its depths. There is more water in Loch Ness than in all the lakes of England and Wales put together, so there is plenty of space to hide!

ISLANDS

Scotland has more than 790 islands. However, many of these islands are very small and nobody lives there. Only 89 islands have people living there all the time.

Mull is one of Scotland's biggest islands, and its largest town is called Tobermory. Find out which children's TV show is filmed in this town.

The Outer Hebrides have lots of white sandy beaches with very clear water. They are some of the most beautiful beaches in the world.

Scotland's islands are mostly split into four large groups. These groups are the Orkney Islands, the Shetland Islands and the Inner and Outer Hebrides.

FACT CAT FACT

Most people in the Outer Hebrides speak **Gaelic** as well as English. Many young people throughout Scotland are now learning to speak Gaelic at school.

FOOD

Scotland's seas, lakes and rivers are home to many different types of fish and **shellfish**. Fish is often smoked, which dries it out. This makes the fish last much longer before it needs to be eaten.

The traditional Scottish way to smoke fish is to hang it over a wood fire that gives out lots of smoke.

Haggis is a traditional Scottish dish. It is made of meat from a sheep, mixed with onion, **oatmeal** and spices. People also eat **vegetarian** haggis, which is made with beans instead of meat.

Haggis is often eaten with 'neeps and tatties'. Find out what the English names for these vegetables are.

neeps

haggis

tatties

FACT CAT FACT

Every year, many people have a special meal to celebrate a famous Scottish poet called Robert Burns. A haggis is carried into the room while music plays, and then one person reads a poem to it!

WILDLIFE

Red squirrels live in the forests of Scotland. There used to be lots of red squirrels in the UK, but now they are quite **rare**. Most of them are found in northern Scotland.

FACT CAT FACT

There are many more grey squirrels than red squirrels in the UK. Grey squirrels eat lots of food that red squirrels need, and they pass on nasty diseases.

Squirrels live high up in trees, in homes made from leaves, twigs and **moss**. Find out what a squirrel's home is called.

The Scottish wildcat looks a lot like a pet cat, but it lives in the wild. It has lived in Scotland for more than 10,000 years – long before people even kept cats as pets!

Today, there are only around 100 Scottish wildcats left. However, people in Scotland are working very hard to **increase** this number.

FESTIVALS

The Edinburgh Festival takes place every summer. It is one of the largest festivals in the world. People can see art, music, **theatre** and **comedy** shows in places all over Edinburgh.

The Edinburgh Festival has more than 2000 shows, as well as many fun events taking place in the streets.

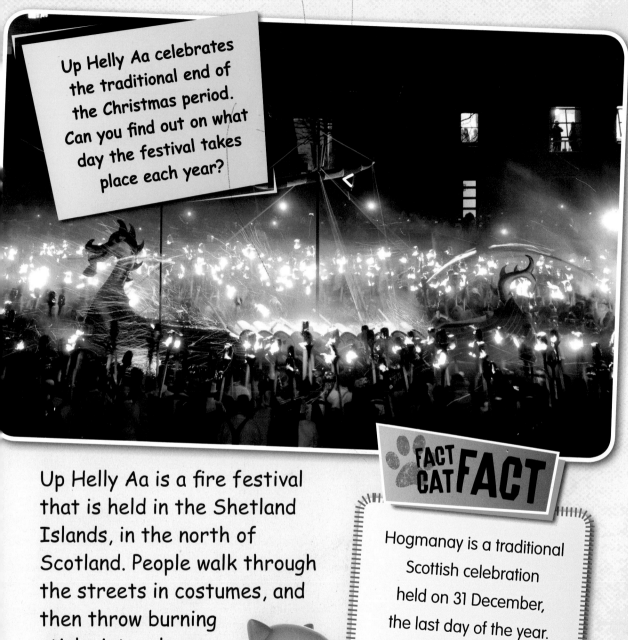

Up Helly Aa celebrates the traditional end of the Christmas period. Can you find out on what day the festival takes place each year?

Up Helly Aa is a fire festival that is held in the Shetland Islands, in the north of Scotland. People walk through the streets in costumes, and then throw burning sticks into a large wooden boat.

FACT CAT FACT

Hogmanay is a traditional Scottish celebration held on 31 December, the last day of the year. At midnight, people hold hands in a circle and sing a song called 'Auld Lang Syne'

FAMOUS PEOPLE

Scottish people have **invented** many things we use today. John Logie Baird created the world's first television around 90 years ago. Alexander Graham Bell invented the telephone around 140 years ago.

Alexander Graham Bell didn't like to have a telephone in his office. He found it annoying when the phone rang as he had to stop work to answer it!

This photograph shows Bell making a telephone call. Find two more things that Scottish people invented.

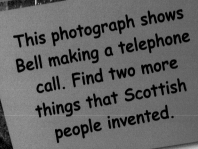

18

Andy Murray is a tennis player from Scotland. He is one of the top players in the world. He has won the men's **singles** title at the US Open and Wimbledon, two of the biggest tennis competitions in the world.

Andy Murray has won over £18 million in prize money from tennis competitions. He also won a gold medal at the 2012 Olympics in London.

SPORT

The most popular sports in Scotland are football, **rugby** and **golf**. The Scottish town of St Andrews is often called 'The Home of Golf'. People have played golf there for more than 600 years.

Scotland has a very good women's curling team. Curling is a sport where players slide stones across the ice at a **target**.

Highland Games are events that celebrate Scottish culture. People take part in traditional sports and dances, and listen to music played on **pipes** and drums.

The caber toss is a Scottish sport in which people pick up and throw a very tall, heavy log. Find out how you score high points in a caber toss.

Highland Games are held all over Scotland, but they also take place in other countries. There are Highland Games in Brazil, Bermuda and Indonesia, which are all very far away from Scotland.

QUIZ

Try to answer the questions below. Look back through the book to help you. Check your answers on page 24.

1 Where in Scotland is the festival of Up Helly Aa held?

a) Mull

b) Shetland Islands

c) Dundee

2 Which Scottish person invented the telephone?

a) John Logie Baird

b) Andy Murray

c) Alexander Graham Bell

3 All of Scotland's islands have people living on them. True or not true?

a) true

b) not true

4 What is the biggest city in Scotland?

a) Glasgow

b) Edinburgh

c) Aberdeen

5 Scottish wildcats have lived in Scotland for more than 10,000 years. True or not true?

a) true

b) not true

GLOSSARY

capital the city where the government (the group of people who lead a country) meets

coat hair or fur that covers the body of an animal

comedy type of entertainment in which performers make people laugh

extinct an extinct volcano no longer has melted rock, called lava, coming out of it

Gaelic language that people in Scotland have spoken for around 1700 years

golf sport in which players use special clubs to hit a small ball into holes in the ground

harbour place on the coast where people can safely leave their ships

increase to make something bigger

invent to make something that has never existed before

moss small plant that has no flowers and grows on trees and rocks as well as the ground

mountain a mountain is taller, and usually more rocky, than a hill

museum building where important objects from history, art and science are kept

oatmeal dried food made from oats, which are part of a plant

rare not found or seen very often

rugby team sport in which players kick, throw or run with the ball

shellfish small animal that lives in water and has its body inside a hard shell

shipyard place where ships are built or repaired

singles type of tennis where two people play against each other

target a place or object that players aim at and try to hit

theatre type of entertainment in which actors perform stories on a stage

tourist person who is visiting somewhere for a holiday

traditional describes something that a group of people have had, done or made the same way for a long time

vegetarian food with no meat in it, for people who don't eat meat

volcano rocky hill around an opening in the Earth's surface, through which melted rock called lava can come out

INDEX

Aberdeen **7**
animals **8, 14–15**

Baird, John Logie **18**
beaches **11**
Bell, Alexander Graham **18**
boats **6, 7, 17**
Burns, Robert **13**

cities **5, 6–7**
coast **7**

Dundee **7**

Edinburgh **5, 6, 16**
England **4, 9**

famous people **18–19**
festivals **16–17**
food **12–13**

Gaelic **11**
Glasgow **6**

Hebrides **11**
Highlands **8–9**
Hogmanay **17**

islands **10–11**

lochs **9**

mountains **4, 8**
Mull **10**
Murray, Andy **19**
music **13, 16, 21**

Northern Ireland **4**
Orkney Islands **11**

River Clyde **6**

Shetland Islands **11, 17**
sport **19, 20–21**
St Andrews **20**

towns **10, 20**

United Kingdom **4**
Up Helly Aa **17**

Wales **4, 9**
wildlife **14–15**

ANSWERS

Pages 6–21

page 6: The Squinty Bridge

page 8: Highland cattle can be black, brindled (black and brown striped), red (the colour shown in the picture on page 8), yellow (pale yellow-brown) and dun (very pale brown).

page 10: Balamory

page 13: The English name for 'neeps' is swede, and 'tatties' are potatoes.

page 14: drey

page 17: the last Tuesday in January

page 18: There are many inventions to choose from. Some examples are: colour photography, flushing toilets, kaleidoscopes, penicillin, raincoats and canals.

page 21: In caber tossing, you don't win points for how far the caber travels. You score high points by throwing the caber so it turns around in the air and lands with the other end facing you.

Quiz answers

1	b)		4	a)
2	c)		5	a)
3	b)			

OTHER TITLES IN THE FACT CAT SERIES...

SPACE

978 0 7502 8220 8

978 0 7502 8221 5

978 0 7502 8222 2

978 0 7502 8223 9

COUNTRIES

978 0 7502 8212 3

978 0 7502 8213 0

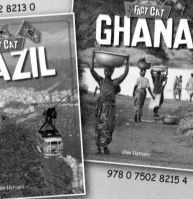

978 0 7502 8215 4

978 0 7502 8214 7

WAYLAND